My First
MOG 123

First published in paperback in Great Britain in 2018 by HarperCollins Children's Books.

1 3 5 7 9 10 8 6 4 2

ISBN: 978-0-00-828264-6

HarperCollins Children's Books is a division of HarperCollins Publishers Ltd.
All text and illustrations © Kerr-Kneale Productions Ltd 1970, 1976, 1980, 1984, 1985, 1986, 1988, 1991, 1993, 1994, 1995, 1996, 2000, 2018
Judith Kerr asserts the moral right to be identified as the author and illustrator of the work.
A CIP catalogue record for this book is available from the British Library. All rights reserved.
No part of this publication may be reproduced, stored in a retrieval system, or transmitted in any form or by any means, electronic, mechanical,
photocopying, recording or otherwise, without the prior permission of HarperCollins Publishers Ltd, 1 London Bridge Street, London SE1 9GF.

www.harpercollins.co.uk

Printed and bound in China

My First
MOG 123

HarperCollins *Children's Books*

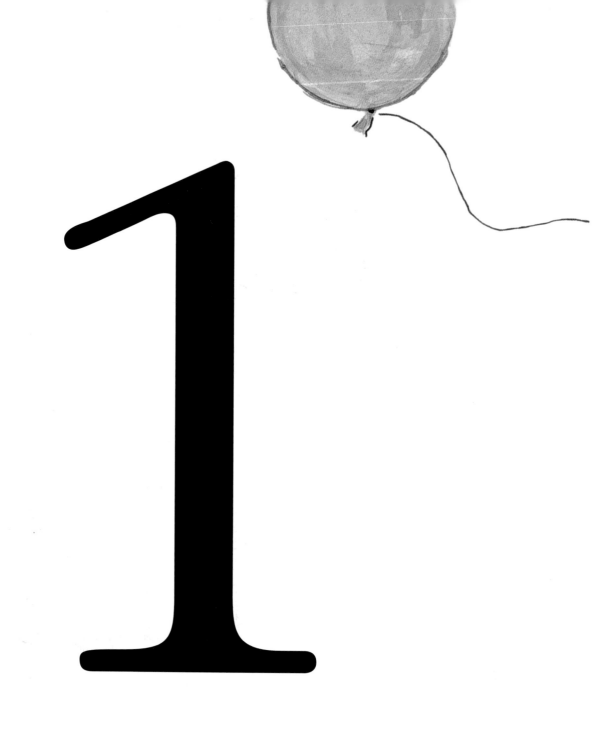

1

One

One Mog.

2

Two

Two children to tickle
Mog's tummy.

3

Three

Three dogs to
chase Mog.

Four

Four people in Mog's
family. And Mog!

Five

Five rainbow mice
in Mog's toy.

6

Six

Six grannies at the party.

7

Seven

Seven butterflies
for Mog to play with.

8

Eight

Eight animals waiting
for the V.E.T. And Mog...

9

Nine

Nine people to watch Mog fly!

10

Ten

Ten mice in Mog's dream.

And a few more on the snow...

1
One

2
Two

3
Three

7
Seven

8
Eight

9
Nine

4
Four

5
Five

6
Six

10
Ten

You can count on MOG for more great adventures!

MOG in the Garden
Judith Kerr

MOG'S Kittens
Judith Kerr

MOG'S Family of Cats
Judith Kerr

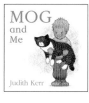

MOG and Me
Judith Kerr

My First MOG ABC
Judith Kerr

MOG and Me and Other Stories
Judith Kerr

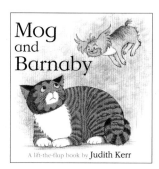

Mog and Barnaby
A lift-the-flap book by Judith Kerr

My First MOG Books
Judith Kerr

Even more Mog titles to take home.

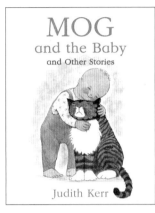

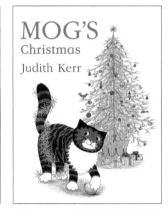

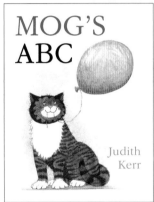

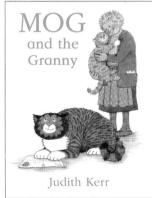

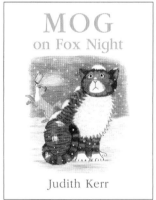

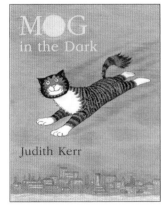